MW01252498

Alphabet Advice

for Adults

From the letters A to Z, introspective words come into being- creating a collection of inspirational writings

R. R. HAYMAN

Copyright © 2014 R. R. Hayman
All rights reserved.

ISBN: 0692027629
ISBN 13: 9780692027622
Library of Congress Control Number: 2014908650

R.R. Hayman, Farmington Hills, Michigan

This book is dedicated to:

The visionaries,
The pioneers,
The foot soldiers in the frontlines,
The underdogs,
The trailblazers—
All who tirelessly fight
To create a
More peaceful world.

Introduction

There are only twenty-six letters in the alphabet we use for English. But with these basic letters, we can assemble extraordinary words, create a rich dialogue, tell a story, speak another language, deliver a message, or sing a song. Through the power of words, opinions can be formed, changed, or revised. *Alphabet Advice for Adults* is a book that offer you hope for the future, and suggestions of how to be a self-advocate. Breaking old patterns of behavior is challenging, but it is then that we can create opportunities for new beginnings. Although we are done learning our ABC's in school, we are never done learning about life's enriching experiences

My advice is real. The content is practical, understandable, and both simple and deep. The catchy phrases make it easier for you to take your "ball of knowledge" and run with it. The diverse writing compositions include poetry, jingles, visual guided imagery, supportive words of encouragement, and much more. Each letter of the alphabet has words of wisdom to share, assembled in diverse writing styles designed to give you, the reader, a morale boost and an extra dose of motivation to take steps toward improving your quality of life.

I hope you take joy in this odyssey of self-discovery as you read through the pages of this book. When you're done reading *Alphabet Advice for Adults*, it is my hope that this book will put a smile on your face, and increase your curiosity to learn more about yourself. Open your heart. Open your mind. How will you embrace your letters today? The ABCs is where we begin.

A

"Awareness"

Why do we give our thoughts so much **attention**? What is a thought, **anyway**? It is a spark of information that flashes and disappears in our heads. When we **attune** our **awareness** to the repetition of these internal ideas, the spark turns into a flame. The flame becomes a wildfire... if we let it.

A thought is made of words. Words enter our **awareness**. Words are made of letters. A thought is just a thought. That's **all** it is. Thoughts clumped together become clusters of thoughts. Why do we let these cognitive experiences **affect** our lives so much? And why do we allow them to form our self-esteem, mold our self-concept, and shape our identities? How do we get so **attached** to our thoughts that we put ourselves **at risk** of **addictive** thinking?

The brain is like a freight train moving in a seemingly continuous state of locomotion. When does a train slow down, come to a stop, and rest? It does when it needs re-fueling. It must. We also must take regular, much-needed breaks so our minds and bodies can recharge. The challenge is that the brain is designed to be an **active** thinking machine. It's up to us to not burn out the battery.

It's time to reclaim the power, which is ours to reclaim, to take charge of our thoughts. We can do this by carefully **analyzing** the relevance of the ideas presented to us and reflecting on the source that created them. Worthy thoughts, proven to be helpful, can be stored in the "files" of your brain. The purposeless thoughts can be "deleted" so there's **additional** storage for vital data. We can even symbolically press the "refresh" button when we feel overloaded.

So why do we get caught up in this messy mind game? For what reason? There isn't any good reason. **After** all, aren't we the conductors of our own trains—the ones in control of what thoughts to embrace and what ones to let go? Every once in a while, we need to slow our wheels down and refill our tanks so we can move full-steam **ahead**.

A

"Transforming Anger"

Sublimated **anger** is sensible anger when it is converted into **action**. Anger can be a useful tool in your toolbox of emotions when you can identify its source. Finding a solution to anger is healing in itself. When not **acknowledged** properly, anger tends to bottle itself up inside. Society has done an excellent job of teaching us that repression is better than expression where anger is concerned. But when anger is bottled up, it festers; it lingers. Perhaps someone is trying to push you down in a relationship, withholding information that could help you get **ahead** in your career, or simply holding you back from excelling in your personal development. Something's bothering you during the day, but you can't quite put your finger on it. It's the anger that you **aren't addressing**.

When you're angry, it's a sign something is wrong. Picking up on this cue allows your brain to go into fix-it mode. Channel that anger into pushing yourself upward and outward from the spot you're stuck in, and get yourself unstuck. Do it just because someone pissed you off! Neutralize your anger by breaking the cycle—by doing something new today. Break out of your stifled state of anger. We are creatures of habit, and if we see anger modeled for us in childhood, we are likely to become angry adults. If we repeatedly get angry, then we are apt to continue to react angrily.

As humans, we cling to the familiar, whether it's working for us or not. Just because behaving a certain way is an established pattern doesn't mean that pattern can't be broken. If we can turn the page of a book, we can also turn the different pages of our lives. Give yourself that permission. The only one holding you back from growth is yourself.

B

Believe you can achieve!

We can discover how people tick by observing animal **behavior**. What does a hunted animal do when it knows a predator is in sight? It freezes. Sometimes it camouflages itself or even plays dead. If the animal wants to avoid becoming prey, it must avoid drawing attention. Self-protection is instinctive. If the animal starts running, the predator would chase it for its next meal. But if the weaker animal stays still, it reduces its chances of being detected.

The bully is like the predator, and the bully's target is the prey. Instead of a mountain lion eating a gazelle for lunch, a bully can eat up all the spirit and goodness in an innocent victim. Consider how we can use the animal kingdom's tactics to protect ourselves from future bullying.

In our culture, we are no strangers to power struggles **between** people. **Bullying** is a prime example and can happen at any age. When a potential victim is nonreactive, bullies can become bored and lose interest in their prey. Psychologically, the bully enters a mindset of being bored or unchallenged. It's when the target of mistreatment shows his or her vulnerability that the power-hierarchy gap widens. **Bottom** line: **be** nonreactive.

The next time someone tries to get under your skin and is on a mission to make you feel like you're two inches tall, ignore it. You will greatly reduce your risk of being the target of bullying. Ask yourself, "Why should I suffer unnecessarily? Why should I let this bullying affect my quality of life? Who's punishing whom?" By letting the bully in, you not only allow the bully to bully but also put yourself in a place of vulnerability.

Set **boundaries** with those you interact with. Keep yourself from internalizing other people's idiotic attempts to make you feel bad. It's their issue—they're acting out and trying to take their own problems out on you. Don't let them. Be clear about how you expect to be treated. You can achieve this by simply being **brave**. There's no need to explain yourself. Be the **best** you can be, and the rest will fall into place.

B

Be like a karate champ; take the **blows** and roll with the punches.

It's up to me to be happy today. I don't have to wait for something **bigger** to come my way in order to experience true joy in the here and now. Why wait?

Life is not a dress rehearsal. This is show time!

C

Consistency + Continuity = Credibility

It is a testament to your strength to be **completely** aligned with your true self, and not veer off on an unintended direction. In the presence of distracting outside influences, you stare at your traveled path with the keenest of your navigational skills. You have laser beam focus on your point of destination. That's **clarity.**

If we get **caught** up with foolishly guessing how much money other people have in the bank, how much love they have in their relationship, or how many square feet their homes are, we get swept away in simplistic thinking. We will never have all the facts to back up our theories of other people's successes or misfortunes. It's a waste of time to bury our heads in business that is not ours. It's not fair to **compare**.

D

"Don't give yourself away for free"

Have you ever lost sight of how special you are after experiencing rejection? It's easy to suffer from low self-esteem when engaging in overanalyzing what has gone wrong. This type of self-**defeating** thinking can make you wind up on the **"discount rack"** which is a symbolism for underestimating your awesome qualities. Whether you're second guessing yourself in a working scenario, or feeling insecure in an interpersonal relationship, psychologically pushing yourself down is **debilitating.**. When you **degrade** what you have to offer, you are symbolically putting yourself on sale.

Instead of thinking you'd be lonely if you don't win the love of a "good catch" or acquire that job promotion you've been hoping for, *reverse your thinking.* Put yourself

11

on a pedestal. Celebrate your authenticity, and stride with confidence. It's never too late to start loving yourself.

Realize that you are getting **distracted** from acknowledging what divine gifts you were born with. You could fulfill your inner calling by embracing your innate qualities. Whenever you rush into some action that stems from an idea you've had, you can get sucked into a limited way of thinking. You get so attached to this idea that this is the way 'it has to be'. Your gut instincts are also your inner voice. Listen to it. It's telling you to be the best that you can be.

Baby, you're not only full price—you are a *limited edition!*

When you feel **drained** from a long, exhausting day of frustration, and you can't help but anticipate tomorrow's unmet challenges, think instead of all of your hard work, and connect with your accomplishments. **Don't** throw away what you've put in today.

In the **depths of despair**, pure joy can be **discovered** if it's sought in the most perfect place. That place is love.

E

"Easy on Yourself"

When you look at your life as a whole—the ups and downs, the big deals and small stuff, the triumph and tribulation—keep in mind that it is you who will ultimately be responsible to care for yourself. You are the only person who gets you up in the morning. You are the person who brushes your teeth. It is you and only you who is born into this world. It you and only you that meets with your maker when the time is right..

When it's all said and done, give yourself the unconditional love that you deserve. Be your own mother, your own father, your own best friend. Ask yourself, "What would my best friend tell me to do in this situation?" When you've found your answer, you will realize that these words will usually point you in the right direction.

If you can think of comforting words to support your friend, you can figure out a way to support yourself. Instead of being your own worst critic, go **easy** on yourself.

Your mind-body-spirit **energy** is like a jar of jelly beans. There are only so many; save them. Use them well. If you waste them, your **extras** won't be there when you really need them. Visualize the different colors of the jelly beans in a clear mason jar. As you see the different colors, try to estimate the number of candies are in the jar. Keep track of the numbers. When you exhaust your energy, the jelly beans disappear. But when you feel exhilarated, you can put some jelly beans back into the jar. Think about how we want to hold on to our energy in the short term, and long term of your life, so pace yourself throughout the life cycle. Try not to let your jar run **empty**.

F

"Far, Far Away"

May the **flowers** of your garden
Be prosperous and nurture
The seeds that germinate life—
Beauty expanding with vibrant colors,
Flowing with the unending,
Blooming gifts of Mother Nature.

Magnificent gardens
Full of life,
Full of wonder,
Fruitful works of art
Stretching **far**
Beyond the physical,
Transcending space and time.

G

"A Grudge is like Gravity"

When you hold a **grudge**, remember: you're the one holding it. If you're sprinting from point A to point B, what backpack would be easier to carry? The backpack holding fifty rocks, or the backpack with fifty feathers?

You know the answer. Lighten your load so you can advance with a **greater** degree of flexibility. Let go of the grudge you're clinging to. Free yourself of your grudge's **gravity**, which has weighed you down for far too long. Live the life you've always dreamed about, and do it with complete forgiveness.

Life isn't always wrapped in a pretty little **gift box** with the perfectly tied bow. People like to think that they can **get through** challenging situations without messiness. Life is messy. If you want to embrace the **giant** within you, be **graceful** enough to roll up your sleeves and get your hands dirty. There are no short cuts. It's time to **get over** your fears, and get past your needs for the keeping things the same. The true gift is there, but it is hidden in the center of the gift box underneath the wrapping, ribbons and bows.

H

"Coming Home"

Be **humble.** Keep both feel planted on the ground, your eyes gazing toward the limitless sky. Remember where you came from, and know where you're going.

Our parents taught us to be **honest** with other people. At the same time, we must not forget to begin by being honest with ourselves.

Human kindness is a word that should at the forefront of your thinking. The word *kindness* is coupled with the word human. This is very significant. Take the time to reflect on this compound word. Is human kindness a word that will be lost and forgotten from the English language? When do you hear people conversing about the art of human kindness? To be human is also to be kind. It's a beautiful word, and it deserves more attention.

To **heal** a broken **heart** is to have **hope** for **happier** times to come.

I

"Illusion"

Your reality is merely an **illustration** of your gathered thoughts, **impressions**, and **ideas** derived from your perception. So, what is reality? It's an **illusion**.

Immerse yourself in the tranquility of the present moment. This moment is unique. There will never be another moment exactly like this one.

Ignite your passion to achieve your **innermost** ambitions.

J

"Jump Up for Joy"

The soul is like a **jigsaw** puzzle, comprising a multitude of complex parts. Some parts may seem to be missing. Most of the pieces are available to us, whether or not we acknowledge they are already there. As we seek to fill the empty spaces, sometimes we find the missing pieces, and sometimes we don't. Being within this emptiness fosters our longing to become more than what we are now.

If all the pieces were neatly placed in front of us, we would be devoid of the kinetic push and pull of life's energy, which is the fundamental ingredient of our existence.

Join me in my **journey** to remind our fellow human beings to

- recycle;
- put the cell phone down during dinnertime;
- visit the sick and the elderly;
- open the door for a stranger;
- put the grocery cart back in its proper place in the parking lot;
- genuinely compliment loved ones;
- say "I love you";
- say "I'm sorry";
- take a "social media" hiatus.

It is our **job** collectively to build a more pleasant, peaceful, and safe world to live in—one interaction at a time. It's important not only to start being more thoughtful today, but also to consider the legacy we are leaving behind for the new generations. Their future and well-being throughout the ages are depending on it.

We may or may not have the privilege of seeing the rewards of our good deeds in this lifetime. In either case, **justice** will always prevail!

K

"Some Kind of Rap"

If your lover treats you anything less than superb,
Do yourself a favor and **kick** 'em to the curb!

When someone really wants you,
he'll **knock** down your door.
No need to act desperate,
you know what you've got in store!

If they start playin' games with your mind,
tell 'em they're not bein' **kind**.

The **key** to someone's heart
is mutual respect, loving, and trust
starting from the start.

Just 'cause you're alone doesn't make you lonely.
Please don't settle for the weirdos or the homely.

Your inner joy is your divine right,
a given constant.
Hold on to it tight.

Protect your dignity like something fierce.
Keep the peace in your temple,
your skin they can't pierce.
Head up, shoulders back,
pick up speed, give your butt a smack!

March forward with **pride**.
May the best of luck be on your side!

L

"L Questions"

Is **luck** for the chosen few?

or

Do we make our own luck based upon the choices we make throughout our **lives**?

When we **lose** something, do we really 'lose' it?

In the big picture, we may **learn** that the **loss** actually led to a gain that only could have happened because of that loss. Perhaps the loss made us learn an important **life lesson** which made us stronger. Maybe that loss taught us a message that we'll pass on to others. Maybe we didn't lose anything, since it was never ours in the first place.

Maybe if we didn't lose that something, we could have never opened ourselves up for that something greater that was waiting for us.

Look around.
See what's been **lost.**
See what's been found.

M

"In a New York Minute"

Sometimes a simple **moment** can turn into a **memory** that can last for a lifetime.

The best **medicine** is a golden retriever.

To some, the **meaning** of a **minute** is one-sixtieth of an hour. To **me**, a minute is sixty seconds that I will **make** count. What will you do with your **magical** minutes today?

What's **mine** is mine; I can selectively share with others. But if I keep everything—my knowledge and time and possessions—to myself, then how will I be aiding the preservation of humankind?

If you **mess** with me; you're **messing** with my history.

N

"Detach from what is No Longer Needed"

You don't **need** to find a solution right this second. Just know that things will get better in time. Acknowledge where you're at in your discontentment. Face your conflict straight on, and have the courage to hold it until it's ready to be let go. We tend to need instant gratification and want to get the answers right away. We know all too well this doesn't always happen. One step at a time, tackle your dilemma. I promise you'll get to where you need to be. Require **nothing** except what is there. Be patient. Take a deep breath.

Give yourself permission to be happy for **no** reason at all.

Why wait for happiness?

Do we **need** to get richer, smarter, or more famous to be happy?

Can we be happy today just because?

After all, who dictates our happiness?

Who put themselves in charge of making our decisions?

Who wrote the handbook of societal **norms**?

We fall into the trap of believing what we're seeing.

Why should we let others affect our mental well-being?

We can't depend on others to bring us up.

We can't allow others to bring us down.

We habitually put ourselves down,

whether we admit it or **not**.

We don't **need** to be that way anymore.

The thing we may regret most

at the end of our lives is not choosing to be happier

when we had the chance.

Be happy doing absolutely **nothing**!

Make your **needs** and desires matter. Surrounding yourself with **nurturing** people will make it easier for you to be well received. Even the most empathic people we encounter are not mind readers. Speak your mind. Articulate your thoughts. You will be more respected by others and experience a raised self-esteem as a result.

N

"The Next Step"

It's **not** that she knows, and doesn't care. She doesn't care to know about it in the first place. Enter the **next** step towards knowing what you care about.

Free yourself from **negativity**.

Although we may not feel that we've gotten everything we've wanted in life, we have the free will to choose **non-complacency**.

O

"Overcoming Obstacles"

Obliterate the younger generation's misconception that they are entitled to adult liberties.

The attribute of being authentic far **outlasts** that fleeting-ness of being fake.

You are born with a genetically inherited set of survival skills. Search deep within yourself to find those abilities that will serve you well in the future. Plug yourself into the process of cultivating your self-awareness. **Overcome** the **obstacles**.

When you're **optimistic** during times of struggle, it's a lot easier on the brain and body than if you **opt** to be stressed out. If optimism is healthier for you than resorting to fear or misery, choose to be optimistic as a prescription for living.

O

"Obligation means Commitment"

Don't be the nautical captain who escapes from his sinking ship on the first rescue boat. The passengers of his ship are counting on him to provide enough rescue boats, and staff assistance in case of a maritime disaster. The passengers enter the ship with the trust that they are protected and safe during their voyage. It is tragic when the captain who has ultimate responsibility for the ship and its passengers would be the first person to jump ship leaving everyone to scramble and survive.

Like the captain of the ship, we are responsible to navigate **our** lives with alertness and long-term vision. Throughout the life cycle, who are all likely to experience some level of disappointment from another person's inability to follow through. We as human beings are striving for improvement in keeping our word, yet we can also be flawed in this area as well. As adults, our bodies may be fully developed, but our minds never stop growing. When we see kids grow up, and watch them turn into adults, we can see their physical growth. It's much harder to grasp the magnitude of how mind continues to evolve over time.

With this in mind, we can work on our weakness, and try to get stronger in spite of our presented limitations. A prime example, is the fulfillment of obligations. When we fail to fulfill our **obligations** to other people, we let them down. Consider how our actions have a direct impact on those around us As we build empathy for others with life experience, we can utilize that sensitivity to act in more thoughtful ways toward others. Some suggestions for improving the fulfillment of obligations:

* use a daily planner
* **organize** different rooms in the home
* reexamine how you budget the time
* be mindful of sleeping and eating patterns
* write down important tasks on a sticky note to reinforce what you are trying to remember.
* engage in mental exercises to jog your memory, and sharpen your thinking

* work on feeling proud of the hard work you're doing and how that hard work is paying off in every area of life.
* be ready to have genuine intentions about improving the fulfillment of obligations
* being kind and respectful to others is a moral obligation. To be kind to **others** is not a choice, it's a must.

P

"Perseverance"

When you feel that you're losing sight of what you're working toward and can't see what all your effort is for—**persevere**. Concentrate closely on what your roadblocks are and how, specifically, you can remove those barriers in order to stay on your intended **path**.

"The 100 Percent Factor"

Close your eyes for a minute. Visualize the number one hundred with a **percent** symbol (%) after it in neon lights. Imagine this number floating right in front of you.

The sign looks like the hot-pink "OPEN" sign you would see at the entrance of a delicatessen.

Ask yourself, "What is my ultimate **purpose?**" When you receive the answer, give it your all; give it 100 percent of yourself. **Picture** your **perfect plan**, and keep this idea in the forefront of your mind.

Try out this method. I think you will be **pleased** with the results. Many of my clients have been.

Turn **pain** into **purpose**.

People are not **possessions**. Relationships are not owned but, rather, should be mindfully managed. A **person** is not a toy—one day a desirable plaything and another day forgotten, discarded at the bottom of the closet. A person has feelings and is bound to feel sadness if deserted and feel confused by mixed messages. That's just not a fair way to treat another human being.

Each person is a gift on loan from our creator, with us on this earth for a fixed **period** of time. We never know how long we have to spend with our loved ones. Value the time you have together. Trying to control each other erodes the beauty of the totality of the shared experience.

Do I **practice** what I **preach**? I'm not **perfect**, but I will **pry** open the gates of resistance.

Q

"Questioning the Status Quo"

Instead of asking yourself the **question**, "How hard has my challenge been on me?" inquire: "How hard am I making this on myself?"

Here is another question to reflect on:

"How is my problem taking control of my life?" Or you could look at it another way and ask, "How can I take control of my problem so my life can get better?"

Remember if it's between you and the problem, never let the problem win. You have the power to find an effective way of coping with the issue. Your **quality** of life warrants your attention.

If you feel stuck in a **quandary**, and you're unsure how to proceed, stop what you're doing! Don't take immediate action if you don't have to. Make a list of the benefits and risks. Ask some friends for advice. Wait a few days to think it over. Then decide what to do. Giving yourself the opportunity to reconsider will help you make smarter choices.

R

"Breaking through Resistance"

It's when we **resist** facing our problems that stress ensues. Plug yourself in to what exactly is going on. Unblock whatever might be holding you back from being proactive.

Connect with your awareness of how you **react** to different situations. **Recognize** that there are a multitude of methods of how you can **respond** to your environment. Find a new way to **relate**.

Reliability is one of the most important attributes one can possess. There are plenty of uncertainties we must face, things that are beyond our control. The least we can do for one another is to be reliable. If we make an effort to try harder to keep our promises, we can improve our integrity. Don't we all want to feel safe and secure with our relationships? Taking personal accountability to become a more reliable person is a **really great place to start.**

It's not our **responsibility** to carry someone else's pain.

Does there have to be a **reason** for everything? Can't it just be?

S

"Sitting in the Shade"

When you want to consciously detach from a thing or person but are having a hard time doing so, try this mental exercise: Imagine a plant that you've tended to, one to which you've given the water and sunlight it needed to thrive. You now discover that this plant is not going to thrive in your home because it was intended to be someone else's.

Now we're going to **switch** gears. It's time to **starve** the plant of all of its necessities for sustaining life. No water. No **sunlight**. No love. No attention.

Although it feels counterintuitive, just go with it. **Step** into a new way of using your imagination. Visualize the plant you once nurtured—now a plant of neglect. Watch the leaves drying, **shriveling**, falling down to the floor, and cracking into tiny pieces. The leaves are so light and **small** that they are flying away with the flow of the air. You look at your planter and see just dirt. No plant. All the **stems** have withered and **shrunk** back and collapsed into nothingness.

Like this unwanted plant, less-than-desirable behaviors, attachments to the wrong priorities, or involvement with toxic people can present challenges in breaking old habits. We must try to rid ourselves of the essential ingredients that lure us into these difficult **situations**. Your plant is gone. Put the image of the old plant somewhere away from your inner consciousness. Take this opportunity to **shift** your focus onto caring for thriving plants that are plush, vital, and beautifully green.

If you want to lighten up your mood while you're on the phone, here's a **suggestion**: try looking in the mirror and **smiling**

It's not the **state** you're in; it's the state of mind you're in. If you think moving to another state will **solve** your problems, but you bring the baggage with you, you will find yourself in the **same** state of mind wherever you go. Move past fears, and open yourself up for fixing your problems with new **solutions** that will work for you.

Look around at your current environment, and explore how you can make it better. That is potentially more practical than **switching** from one place to another, constantly on the go. What's more helpful is to **surround** yourself with **supportive** people who are like-minded. Look for **strong** mentors who inspire you. And pass on the gift of knowledge—be a mentor yourself. Help reinforce the **significance** of building a powerful teamwork mentality in your local communities. When you help create this framework, you will be the first to reap the benefits.

T

"Take it Full Circle"

Do you want the **truth**? Ask me for the proof!

When we invest our energy in making money, we hope it will be worth our time. **Time** can be the most precious commodity of all.

You don't have to follow a **trend** to become somebody's friend.

The way a **theory** can become a fact begins with **talking** to people about your observations. Be an individual and communicate your ideas without fear of judgment. Your belief is your **truth**. Silence leads to theories becoming weightless in value.

Joining a **team** of "theorists" who unanimously agree in a common goal will help validate the need for research with greater magnitude. Building a strong **teamwork** effort will jumpstart the drive to get the message out to the public. Being a bystander further perpetuates the homeostasis of society's complacency.

To make a theory a fact takes courage. It is factual knowledge that will give your direction to carry on through the life cycle with more confidence. Spreading fact-based information with members of your community is the key to creating a brighter future.

It's not ok to **treat** me this way.

U

"Unlimited"

Imagine coming home from the toy store with a brand new Rubik's Cube. You take it out of the box, and observe it in its original form. The Rubik's Cube has six sides, with six different colors. When you hold it at a certain angle, you can only see the red and green sides. You can't see the blue and orange sides unless you turn the cube in a different direction. Point being that, as with the Rubik's Cube, you can discover new ways to perceive your life challenges by looking at them from different angles. The first step is to "turn the cube" in a different position in order to see the sides you can't see now. Although the

Rubik's Cube has six sides and six colors, the number of times you have to see things in a new light is **unlimited**.

When the weight of your burden seems to be dragging you down, search deeply inside your mind, body, and soul to unleash the mysterious powers that can **uplift** your mood. All that you need to make this happen already lies within you and is waiting for you. Find the determination and tenacity to access these traits. Find the wherewithal to tap into the possibilities to heal yourself from the inside out, rather than the outside in.

Daily meditation and yoga are highly **useful** to achieve this particular goal. If you're a beginner at meditation and would like to find a place to start, I recommend the book, *Wherever You Are, There You Are* by Jon Kabat-Zinn.

Today is **unique**. Accept that the information you have to work with is what you have. Don't let your mind wander onto the 'what if's' which you have no control over. If you can't find more than what you're looking for in the **uniqueness** of today, then you may not be ready to receive that insight just yet. With the art of patience, you will discover that the answers will appear to you when you are ready to receive them.

U

"Untouchable"

When you're around difficult people, imagine there is a Hula-Hoop surrounding you with the greatest of protection. Imagine this hula-hoop is like an invisible force field of protective energy not only surrounding you horizontally, but also vertically. Inside the Hula-Hoop is your personal space, which should be honored by you. Setting this boundary sends out a message: "You can only get so close to me. This is my time, my space, my being that needs some distance right now. Please respect that."

This metaphorical Hula-Hoop only allows positive energy to penetrate. This ring of protection is impermeable when it comes to negative energy. When others try to make you feel **uncomfortable** in any way, the negative energy is repelled by the Hula-Hoop, which shoots the **unwanted** discomfort back to its source.

Then, you're **untouchable**!

V

"Victorious"

Speak your **voice**—loud and clear.
Let the world know you are here!

Validation from others is a bonus but not an entitlement. When you know you've done something right, validating yourself privately is one of the best gifts you can give yourself. And it's free!

Just say the word "**victorious**." Isn't it fun to say? **Visualize** yourself celebrating your **victory** over anything. It could be as simple as cleaning out your garage or buying the last hot sale item left in the store.

The next step is to customize this technique to your personal needs. Link up this state of motivation you're feeling right now with your desired goal. Find that tiger within you who's got the spark of curiosity in your eyes and a **voracious** appetite for the sweet anticipation of victory!

W

"The WIFM Mindset"

The **WIFM** mindset-What's In It For Me?- is an acronym well known in corporate America. The WIFM mindset is spread over to mainstream culture. Unfortunately, we are seeing more and more that people looking out for their own gain, while overlooking the welfare others. Why are we becoming a more selfish people? Together, we must collaborate our ideas, and search for solutions to this pervasive problem.

As a global society, we must continue the quest to fight for nice people to stay nice and for anyone on the fence who is debating between being nice or otherwise to lean on the side of niceness. We are living in an ever-changing **world,** with technology progressing every day, uncertainty in the state of health care, economic and job insecurity, and unending lists of responsibilities to tackle. The change and uncertainty of life can be stressful, and stressed people aren't always their nicest selves.

The competitive nature of today's world has resulted in a sharp decline in generosity to our neighbors. A little healthy competition is a good thing when it lights a fire under us to be passionate about our work. But to be a true **winner**, don't just think of what's in it for you. Yes, we need to look out for ourselves. But we must look out for others too. When we share our secrets for attaining our success with others, we are paying it forward.

X

"Xanadu"

Xanadu is a classically romantic, musical fantasy film from the 1980's. The lead role is played by the famous actress and talented music artist, Olivia Newton-John. Xanadu is one of those movies children and teens of the disco era enjoyed watching countless times.

The music from *Xanadu* is played by the British rock band ELO featuring one of their popular songs, "I'm Alive." This whimsical production is creative movie that can allow your imagination run free from the commotion of everyday life. When do you give yourself the opportunity to relax your mind while viewing the culmination of art, music acting synthesized together? It's time to shift your thinking about the ordinary and enter the world of the extraordinary.

Xanadu is defined as an idyllic, exotic, and luxurious place.

Today, where do you let your imagination go? Allowing the mind to be free to fantasize is healthy. Give yourself permission to imagine a place that is wherever and however you'd wish it to be—a beautiful summer's day on the beach, a field of ruby-red roses, an open, emerald-green pasture—the sky's the limit when it comes to letting your mind go. Take a natural and needed break from the stress, chaos, and constant thinking.

Take a few moments, and experience your own **Xanadu**.

Y

"Life in a Year"

Quit your **yakkin'**, and let's see some action!

If you want to enhance the quality of your life but do absolutely nothing about it, then absolutely nothing will change. Imagine **yourself** exactly one **year** from now. What do you see? The same thing you're doing today? How does that make you feel? Motivated? Enlightened? Determined? Next time you need a little push to get headed in the right direction, think ahead. Get time savvy, why don't **ya**?

Z

"To Zenith and Beyond"

The person with **zeal** will have the greatest appeal.
If she has **zest**, she'll be a cut above the rest!
But if she's too **zany**, she may not be brainy.
So, if she wants to be a hero, she's gotta shoot above **zero**.

34437981R10049

Made in the USA
Charleston, SC
09 October 2014